The Rainbow Story of

Saint Francis of Assisi

Written by Dorothy Smith

Illustrated by Robert Broomfield

McCRIMMONS

For LUKE
with love

First published in Great Britain in 1987 by
McCrimmon Publishing Co Ltd
Great Wakering Essex England

© 1987 Dorothy Smith

ISBN 0 85597 394 3

Cover design Robert Broomfield

Typeset and printed in Hong Kong by
Permanent Typesetting and Printing Co Ltd

Contents

1. The poor man of Assisi

Little Frenchy

EIGHT HUNDRED years ago a boy was born like a prince in a fairy tale, to be showered by the good fairies with gifts at his christening. He had loving parents and a devoted family.

They lived in a beautiful town in Italy, where they were well liked and respected. His father was one of the wealthiest men of the town. The boy himself was lively, healthy and intelligent, with a tremendous charm that made him many friends who accepted him as their leader.

His story tells how he threw all these gifts away, in exchange for something better.

Centuries later his name is known everywhere, and he is greatly loved—though his name was a nickname and he was one of the poorest men who has ever lived. His name was Francis.

He was born in the Italian town of Assisi. In the years when Francis lived there, Assisi was a grey stone city set on a hill. It was crossed by narrow, twisted streets and steep alleyways, and it was protected by a stone wall. Vines and fruit trees spilled down the stony hillside, and away into the blue distance stretched the wide plain of the district called Umbria. Other towns lay twenty or thirty miles away, but they were separate worlds. The citizens of Perugia or Spoleto were foreigners to the people of Assisi—foreigners with whom they were often at war!

Assisi was a thriving town. After they had fed themselves and their families, many people still had money to spend; so the merchants were a prosperous set of men, pleased with the town and themselves.

Pietro Bernadone was a cloth merchant of Assisi. He sold sumptuous velvets and brocades, gleaming damask and soft silk for rich men and their wives and daughters to make into clothes, or for the religious to give to the church for vestments or altar cloths. He took his cloths to fairs and markets all over Italy, and he journeyed even further to find traders who could sell him these treasures. He loved the soft shiny fabrics, both because they were beautiful and because they made him a rich, respected citizen of Assisi.

His favourite journey was always to Provence, in the South of France. There he was received as an honoured guest by nobles in their castles; he was invited to dinner with them, and to listen to the songs of wandering musicians, called troubadours.

At the castle of the Count of Boulevent, Pietro met the Count's daughter, the Lady Pica. He married her and took her back with him to Assisi.

They lived in a house with a warehouse near the market, surrounded by the noise and bustle of customers and passers-by. But Pica may still have been lonely, because she was a foreigner far from home. Provence was a place of singing and music, and she remembered the songs of the troubadours as they wandered from castle to castle, from village to village—songs of heroic tales of adventure, or love songs about beautiful ladies. She sang them over softly to herself.

Pietro still had to carry on his business journeys, and he was away in France when Pica was expecting her first baby to be born. For a while she waited in the stable next to the house so that she could pray to Our Lady, who had had her baby in a stable. At last a baby boy was born, and she had him named John, after John the Baptist, who had told people about the coming of Jesus.

When Pietro came home he was delighted with his son, and he gave him a nickname. Because his mother was French, and because he himself had been away in France when the baby was born, he called the boy his little Frenchman—Frenchy. In Italy, all his life and after, he was called Francesco.

As he became famous, his name was translated into every language in Europe, and in every one of them his nickname has become a favourite boys' name ever since.

So in English we call him Francis.

2. The rich young man

FRANCIS LIKED being known in Assisi as the little Frenchman. His mother taught him the French language and encouraged him to love music. Especially she taught him the songs and ballads the troubadours sang as they travelled through her own Provencal countryside. Soon Francis loved them as much as she did. All his life he was a great singer, and he looked forward to finding a beautiful lady to serve.

His father was proud of his eldest son. As he grew older, and wore doublets of richer cloth, tunics with more embroidery and wider sleeves than any of the other young men of Assisi, Pietro felt young Francis was his greatest achievement.

Rich, well-dressed, a musician, with interesting foreign ways, warm and friendly to everyone he met, young Francis was a natural leader. Even the sons of the local noblemen looked up to him, Pietro Bernadone told his wife proudly.

Francis liked to be admired, but he wanted it to be for some good reason, not just for wearing smart clothes. He felt he had done nothing to deserve admiration so far, and he wanted to do something splendid for his city. Perhaps one day he would even be famous throughout Italy.

The obvious life ahead of him was to become a merchant like his father—but that did not appeal to him. He loved the beautiful fabrics, but he didn't enjoy buying and selling them, and he got into terrible muddles whenever he had to deal with money.

Perhaps he could be a great soldier? The troubadours sang songs of knightly deeds in battle: he wondered if that was the way ahead for him. He soon had a chance of finding out.

In the year 1202, when Francis was twenty years old, the rumbling quarrel between Assisi and Perugia broke out into open war. The young men of the two neighbouring cities rushed out to defend the honour of their home town, and Francis went eagerly with his companions from Assisi.

There was a day of fighting. It was scarcely a battle, more an angry tussle between armed and untrained bands of lads. But some of them were really hurt, and after the day was over some of them had really been taken prisoner. They were taken back to Perugia, forced to parade through the town, and then thrown into prison.

Francis was one of them. It was a wretched end to all his high hopes, shut in a cold, dark fortress with his companions—no longer bold warriors but a huddle of frightened boys—not knowing what was going to happen to them.

Francis bore it well. He kept cheerful and lively, and did not complain of the harsh life, such a contrast to the comforts he had known at home. In fact he was amazed to find he could live without smart clothes and good food and a comfortable bed. He sang his songs; and when the others asked him whatever he had got to be so cheerful about, he laughed.

'Why shouldn't I be cheerful? One day the whole world will bow down to me!'

One of the young men in prison was not accepted by the rest. Whether he had shown fear in the battle or was just unpopular has been forgotten, but the others scarcely spoke to him. Years afterwards they all remembered that Francis had sought this fellow prisoner out and made a friend of him.

They were all in their grim prison for a year. Then peace was patched up between the neighbours, their fathers paid the ransoms agreed on, and the young men went back home.

Reaction and prison conditions made Francis ill. He was struck down with a fever, and it was a long time before he could move about the town and look over the countryside he had missed so much in prison.

He was more thoughtful now than he used to be. Life seemed empty and meaningless, and he was looking for something to fill it. He had not given up his dreams of becoming a famous warrior—the kind of warrior who was celebrated in the songs the troubadours sang. Just once more, for the last time, he set out to try.

A war was breaking out in Italy, not just a skirmish between two towns but a war to drive German invaders out of southern Italy. A local nobleman was forming a troop of cavalry to go and fight, and he called for volunteers. Francis joined eagerly; it seemed a challenging adventure for him. His father bought him horse and armour and equipment, all of the best quality. Francis was very excited, and the night before they were due to set out he had a dream.

He dreamt that as he was standing in his father's shop, with all the rolls of material about him, it changed and became the palace of a beautiful princess. All the cloth became armour, shields, helmets, swords—and in his dream Francis knew the palace and the fair lady and the armour were for him and his followers. Somewhere it was waiting for him.

The next day they rode off. All the townspeople stood at the town gates, or climbed on the city walls, to cheer them on their way to high adventure.

Within a week Francis was back. No one has ever found out why. Was he ill again? Had the nobles in the troop rejected the merchant's son? Had he suddenly realized that for him the road to war was not the way to glory?

It was a terrible return. His father was angry, his mother was completely confused. Everyone in Assisi felt let down and disappointed with the young man who had set out so proudly and happily a few days before.

Francis felt let down and disappointed with himself, but he was certain his way forward would soon be made clear to him. And, like a road gradually appearing in the early morning as the darkness fades and the mists clear, he had a glimmer of an idea where that road might take him.

3. Signposts

FRANCIS ALWAYS loved the countryside around Assisi, especially the high places looking down on the town and the valley below. Even in his most fun-loving days he had liked to get away on his own sometimes. Now, uncertain of himself, he drifted to his favourite haunts and stopped to pray there, at first uncertainly, then with more and more certainty that if there was a way ahead God would make it clear to him.

The churches in Assisi, with their festivals and processions, were part of his life. He went further: he loved Christ, and was deeply moved by the stories of Christ's sufferings throughout his life on earth.

He began to think of the men and women who had given up everything to be Christ's followers on earth. And he thought of one who had not—the rich young man in the story in St Matthew's Gospel.

This young man asked Jesus: 'What good deed must I do to have eternal life?'

Jesus reminded him of the commandments laid down in the Jewish law, but the young man felt there was something else he ought to do.

'All these I have observed. What do I still lack?' he urged.

So Jesus told him what perhaps he knew in his heart already:

'If you would be perfect, go, sell what you possess and give to the poor, and you will have treasure in Heaven; and come, and follow me.'

When the young man heard this he went away sorrowful, for he had great possessions.

And Jesus said to his disciples: 'Truly, I say to you, it will be hard for a rich man to enter the kingdom of Heaven."

Was this meant for *him*? Francis wondered.

He would have said, truthfully, that he loved God and his fellow men. He was charitable to the poor— but he was not made any poorer himself by it. Was he really meant to give up *everything*—to become poor himself?

To be poor, really poor, meant wearing rags, eating scraps, never getting clean, living rough. Surely not!

Then one night, once more out with his friends, in a sudden flash he saw what that meant. Christ himself had given up everything and had actually chosen to be poor because he loved all men and would not own anything that they did not.

In that flash, Francis saw that to be like the poor was to be like Christ.

He stood speechless, so that the others laughed at him and asked if he had fallen in love. Francis laughed, too. 'Yes,' he said, 'I am in love with a bride richer and more beautiful than anyone can imagine. She is called the Lady Poverty!'

So if the path ahead was the service of God, that must mean the service of the poor. Yet even now he did not know how far he was being called to go.

In the Gospels there are stories of Christ healing men suffering from leprosy. This was a hideous deforming disease, so infectious that every reasonable man or woman fled from it. A leper was thrust outside his village, a bell round his neck to give warning of his approach, knowing he must live out his life shunned by everyone except his fellow lepers.

These unhappy souls grouped together. Sometimes a few heroic monks from one of the religious orders would try to care for them.

Leprosy raged across Europe for centuries. In the time of Francis there was a group of lepers living a few miles from the town gates. If ever Francis saw one of them, he was always desperately sorry for him—and desperately afraid of him. He would toss the man a coin, with his head turned away.

Now, with his new ideas stirring him to the depths, one day in the way ahead he saw a leper. He knew this time a coin thrown to the leper was not enough. Terrified, he forced himself to act as he believed Christ would have acted.

He got down from his horse, slowly walked towards the leper and put money actually in his hand. Then he took that scarred and deformed hand, raised it to his lips and kissed it.

It took more courage than facing all the armies of Italy, but he was filled with content. He had seen clearly what God was calling him to do, and he had done it.

He began going each day to a little church on the outskirts of Assisi called St Damian's. The church was in ruins: its roof had fallen in, and though a priest had charge of it, hardly anyone ever stopped there.

Yet there was still an altar inside, and over it hung an old and beautiful crucifix, a figure of Christ painted on a cross of wood. Francis used to kneel before it, his eyes fixed on the figure, thinking of the crucifixion and what it had meant for the world, and begging for a sign to tell him how he was to serve God.

Then one day he heard a clear command that filled the church. It seemed to him that the figure on the crucifix had actually spoken to him.

'Francis,' he heard. 'My house is in ruins. Restore it for me!'

Francis looked around him. Certainly the little church was in ruins. Was that what was meant? Or was he being told that the Church of God itself, throughout all lands, lay in ruins and it was his task to restore it?

Well, that might come later, but St Damian's was certainly in ruins and he could do something about it.

He hurried back to the town. He would need money to buy stone and to pay for workmen.

He went straight to his father's shop and seized several of the best rolls of cloth. He loaded them on his horse and took them to a nearby town. He made the sign of the cross over them, to show they were being used for God's work, and sold them all. Then he sold his own horse as well. He had never been good at buying and selling, and he probably let them all go at bargain prices.

Then, tired but pleased to have carried out the first stage of his work, he traipsed back to Assisi on foot.

His father was absolutely furious. He demanded the money back from selling his cloth, but Francis refused because it was already given to God. So Pietro asserted all the authority a father was allowed in those days. He beat Francis and locked him up in a cellar until he should learn sense.

Francis escaped—perhaps his mother unlocked the door while his father was away—and went to the hillside behind St Damian's and hid in a cave.

He was called out by a special messenger from the Bishop of Assisi, who declared that he would decide in this quarrel between father and son. Francis was quite ready to go.

'I will come before the Lord Bishop gladly, for he is the father and lord of souls,' he said.

He dressed himself in one of his suits of fine clothes and appeared before the Bishop, along with his father and most of the townspeople of Assisi as interested spectators.

The Bishop told Francis firmly that the cloth was not his to take and the money was not his to keep, but he spoke encouragingly.

'Have faith in the Lord, my son, and fear not, for he himself will be your helper and give you all you need to work for his church.'

Francis saw that this was right. He tossed the money to his father's feet, then astonished everybody by taking off his brilliant and elegant clothes. He tossed these, too, at his father's feet. For the last time he took off the clothes of a rich young man. Then he turned to the crowd, where everybody was staring in amazement.

'Listen, everyone,' he called. 'I am not only giving back gladly the money to the one it belonged to—I am giving back my clothes as well. Until now I have called Pietro Bernadone my father. Now I

will only say Our Father, who art in Heaven!'

He stood up in front of them wearing just his undershirt. The Bishop stood up, too, and with a gesture as dramatic and symbolic as Francis's he threw his own cloak around him.

The Church was giving Francis the shelter he needed.

4. *The little poor man*

THE BISHOP took Francis away and found him some clothes—a labourer's cast-offs: a short tunic, breeches and clumsy felt boots. Francis chalked a cross on the front of his tunic, then set off for St Damian's and asked the priest if he might sleep there while he rebuilt the church.

His immediate problem was how to do that without money. How could he buy building materials or pay labourers? The obvious answer was to ask people to give him stones and do the building himself.

He tried begging for stones in Assisi, and found people unexpectedly helpful. They thought he was mad, but when they remembered the well-dressed rich young man who had ridden off to fight, they felt sorry for him.

Francis himself was just as friendly and cheerful as he had always been. He accepted stones for building, or money to buy stones, or offers of a couple of hours' work, gratefully. He told the givers they were laying up rewards for themselves in Heaven.

So the work went forward. The old priest

thought Francis was working too hard, and tried to help by having a good meal ready for him every evening. After a while this troubled Francis: this was not serving Lady Poverty or trusting in God to provide everything he needed.

He decided he must beg for his bread, just as he begged for the stones. He must actually go out through the streets and knock at back doors and ask for left-overs from the table, or kitchen scraps such as prosperous households flung out to the poorest of mankind.

At first he hated the idea. Then, when he had done it once and sat down to eat his collection of scraps, he felt better. This was indeed living like the poorest and trusting in God to provide for him as he provided for the birds.

He called food given like this 'The Lord's table', and made up his mind that he would always beg for his food from day to day, never owning supplies of food or the money to buy it.

Years later he sat beside a stream with a companion, eating some food they had been given and said: 'This is what I call riches, when we have nothing but what is given by God's providence, like this fine stone table and this clear water, and this bread that we have begged!'

Before long St Damian's was finished. But Francis had discovered another church that was falling down, not far from the settlement where the lepers lived. He visited them every day, and between visits he rebuilt that church too.

Then one day, wandering in the woods in the valley below Assisi, he came upon a ruined chapel in a clearing in the woodland. He had heard of it: there had once been a tiny Benedictine monastery here, with a church they called St Mary of the Angels. The monks had called the little plot of land that held the church and monastery the Little Portion— the Portiuncula. The monks had long ago been recalled to their parent monastery; now brambles and nettles grew up to the walls of the chapel and the clearing was strewn with stones that had fallen from the collapsing walls. It looked as if no services were ever held in the church.

Francis thought it was beautiful—so far from any other building, surrounded by trees and singing birds, devoted to the praise of God. He was certain the place was somehow important for him. He set to work, cutting back the choking undergrowth. Soon he was working all day at the Portiuncula, after visiting the lepers, and sleeping there at night.

He was alone with God, and very happy.

The Portiuncula and St Damian's were important places in the story of St Francis, till his death and long afterwards, and the many pilgrims to Assisi are able to see them.

One morning, after the chapel had been completely restored, a friendly priest agreed to say Mass there, just for Francis, with Francis as his server.

It was St Matthias's Day—February 24th, 1209. Francis was twenty-seven years old. For the Gospel for the day, the priest read:

'Preach, saying the kingdom of Heaven is at hand. Heal the sick, cleanse the lepers, raise the dead, cast out devils: freely ye have received, freely give. Provide neither gold, nor silver, nor brass in your purses, nor scrip for your journey, neither two coats, neither shoes, nor yet staves . . .'

The words struck Francis like a flash of lightning. These were the very words with which Christ had sent his followers out into the world.

'This is meant for me, too,' he thought.

After the Mass he asked the priest to go over the words again with him, and he learnt them by heart. The rest of the day he spent getting ready.

He took off his sandals, his belt and wallet, and his short labourer's tunic. Out of sackcloth he made himself a long gown with wide sleeves, shaped like a cross. He found a rope and tied it round his waist.

As he prepared he sang praises to God, who had shown him the way. He would do as the Disciples had done—and as Christ had done.

He would preach the good news to all people, like Christ. He would care for the sick, the lepers, the outcast, like Christ. And he would be absolutely poor, begging his bread, owning nothing but the clothes he stood up in, like Christ.

As he set out barefoot along the stony roads to preach to all men about the love of God, he gave himself a new nickname.

He called himself Il Poverello—the Little Poor Man.

5. The Brothers

ALL HIS LIFE Francis had possessed great charm and liveliness. He loved singing and making jokes. People took to him, often startled at first by what he had to say, but drawn to the man himself. In all the records of him, no one who met him face to face turned against him except his own father, who could not forgive him for not being the kind of son he himself had wanted.

At this time, Francis was described like this: 'He was of middle height, inclined to shortness. His face was long and prominent, cheerful and kindly; his eyes were black, his hair dark, his nose symmetrical, his lips thin and fine, his teeth white and even, his beard black and rather scanty, his hands thin with long fingers, and his voice powerful, sweet-toned, clear and sonorous.'

With these gifts, Francis made a powerful preacher. People flocked to hear him, at first curious and mocking, but staying to listen. His words were not like the sermons they heard in the churches, stiff and forbidding, setting out the authority of the Church, or limp and feeble attempts to ask for alms for the Church.

Francis spoke vividly, eagerly, passionately, about hope, and faith in God, and about the love of God. He spoke of Christ's teaching, his works of healing, and particularly his sufferings at the end, all showing his love for mankind.

All his hearers listened fascinated. Some went away remembering his words, determined to show more faith, more hope, more love in their own lives—and probably some of them succeeded, for a while.

But some of them considered how Francis had given up the whole of this life to doing just that, and wondered if they had the courage and resolve to do the same. Some of these, one by one, came to him and asked to share his life.

The first two could certainly not be written off as reckless young men dropping out of society. They were middle aged, respected men of substance. Bernard da Quintavilli was a business man; Peter Cathinii was a lawyer and scholar.

Bernard used to go to Francis to talk to him, and he invited him to his own home. One night, secretly, he watched Francis as he knelt in prayer, and he was overcome by his absorption and his devotion. This finally decided him to take the plunge. He sold all his goods and went to the town square, and began giving all the money to the poor, to the sick, to the clergy for their churches.

Francis helped him do this—and it seems to have been the last time in his life he ever handled money. It was like a great party. But there was one gloomy face, a priest called Sylvester who had sold Francis some stones for his building work very cheaply.

He complained indignantly: "You said you had no money to pay for my stones! You can give me some of all this money, to make up!'

Francis agreed immediately, and pushed a handful of money into the priest's hands.

'Is that enough?' he asked, and Sylvester, rather taken aback, agreed that it was, and went home.

Ever afterwards, Francis would call Bernard his eldest son, because he was the first of his followers. But Peter was not long behind. They went to Portiuncula and made themselves a hut with branches and bracken from the wood. Bernard and Peter got themselves long habits, shaped like a cross, like the one Francis wore, and they praised God together and asked him to bless their new lives.

One young man had heard Francis preach, and had seen Bernard give away his money. He had very little to give away—he was just the son of a poor farmer—but he longed to serve God as they were doing. He did not know where to find them, but he walked along the road towards the leper settlement and met Francis coming out of the woods. He ran to meet him, and knelt at his feet.

'Brother Francis,' he begged. 'For the love of God, let me join you and the others!'

Joyfully Francis agreed, and took him back to the others. 'Look!' he called. 'Come and see what a good brother the Lord has sent us!'

He was indeed a good brother. He was known as Brother Giles; and whenever the tales of the early days of Francis and his companions are told, Giles the farmer's boy is remembered.

One day they heard footsteps on the pathway through the woods and saw a man drawing closer to them. It was Sylvester the priest. He had been ashamed of his own greed, compared with Francis's generosity, and he understood what Francis meant when he said possessions hardened men's hearts and kept them from God. He wanted to give up his church and parish, and his comforts, and join them, preaching the Gospel to the poor.

They were delighted that a priest had joined them, because he was able to say Mass for them, at St Damian's and Portiuncula.

Others came, as well. Angelo Tancredi was a gentleman and a knight entitled to bear arms. He really had won fame by his courage in battle, as Francis had dreamt of years before. Now he gave up his sword, his horse and his armour to follow Francis.

Leo was one of his closest followers. He may have been a friend of Francis when they were boys; and he was devoted to him. His name means Lion, but he was a very gentle person and Francis used to call him his Little Sheep. Leo could write, and he acted as secretary to Francis, and wrote letters for him if he needed them. He kept records of everything Francis said and did; so we should be very grateful to Brother Leo.

Now Francis was not alone. Some of the brothers went out preaching; some went out working in exchange for food; others visited the lepers. Even so, if they were really to rebuild the church, as the figure on the cross at St Damian's had said, it was a giant task, and Francis had moments of great doubt about what to do next. Then one day he had one of his dreams that were like glimpses into the future.

'I have seen,' he told the brothers, 'great flocks of men coming to us, wanting to put on our habit and follow our rule. I have seen the roads from all nations full of men coming here. The French are coming, the Spanish are hurrying towards us, the Germans and the English come running, and a great crowd of men speaking other tongues.'

6. *The Rule*

THIS VISION, as well as the ever growing number of brothers, showed Francis he must have authority for them and their way of life before they ran into trouble. Already people were asking questions about them.

Who are they? Who says they can preach out in the open air? Are they really allowed to beg from everybody? Is it all right for them to go wandering across the countryside with no proper homes?

Francis determined to go to the top. He decided to go to Rome, to explain things to the Pope, who, he was sure, would understand what they were trying to do and allow them to carry on.

They worked out what they would say to him. They chose to be called the Friars Minor—the Lesser Brothers—to separate them from the great ones of the earth. They wanted to be free to wander from place to place, preaching. And they wanted to be free from owning any property, either as an order or as separate individuals. Francis wrote out the Rule they begged to be allowed to follow.

The Pope, Innocent III, was a man of authority and power. Kings were afraid of him, and waited for him to make his decisions on the great affairs of state. But Francis was sure he would give his attention to the affairs of a group of a dozen men claiming to belong to an unknown order.

When they reached Rome, Francis made his way to the palace where the Pope lived and waited in the corridor where he might pass. Travel-stained, barefoot, in his old habit, Francis was a strange contrast to the bishops and cardinals in their robes, and the richly dressed ambassadors who brought messages from their kings.

At first it was as might have been expected. When the Pope appeared, and Francis tried to speak to him, the Pope cut him short and told him to go away.

Francis was disappointed, but went away thinking God would find another way. Immediately he met the Bishop of Assisi, who had always been kind to him. He had not known the Bishop was in Rome.

The Bishop promised to take him back to the Pope the next day, to speak for him.

So next day Francis read out his Rule to the Pope and his cardinals. He explained that they wanted no permanent shelter and only the food they could beg. They did not want to join any order of monks that existed already, where they would be obliged to stay in one monastery, and where, although the monks gave up all their own possessions, the order itself owned buildings and land and often became rich.

The Friars Minors asked for absolute poverty, and the right to preach the Gospel and help the poor, the sick, the lepers and the outcasts of society.

The Pope feared such a rule was too hard for ordinary men and was certain to fail.

Then a cardinal said: 'This is the way of life Christ commanded for his followers. Dare we say that it is impossible for ordinary men to accept it?'

Then, as the Pope was still doubtful, he declared: 'I believe the Lord intends to use this man, to renew the faith all over the world!'

So now the Pope sent Francis away, but he told him to come back, saying: 'My son, go and pray to Jesus Christ to show us his will.'

That night the Pope had a dream. He believed he saw one of the greatest churches of Rome tottering, with great cracks in its walls, about to crumble into ruin. In his dream he could do nothing to prevent it; not even call out for help.

Then, still dreaming, he saw a barefoot travel-stained man wearing a long grey habit, a rope round his waist—the man who had pleaded with him that day. He stepped forward and stood by the walls of the church until they rested on his shoulder. Then the walls straightened, the cracks mended and the church stood as good as new. In another way, God had called Francis to rebuild his church.

So next day the Pope told Francis he now believed his rule was God's wish, and he would give him authority for it.

He declared the brothers were free to follow their path of poverty, and they were allowed to preach, urging men to love God, give up evil and repent of their sins. Francis was made a deacon in the church, and his companions promised him obedience on behalf of all the brothers.

'Go forth with the Lord, Brothers,' commanded the Pope. "Preach repentance as the Lord inspires you. If your fellowship grows, come back to us and I will grant you more power.'

Innocent III knew he was a great Pope whose name would live in history. He would have been amazed to learn that his greatest claim to fame is the fact that he authorised Francis of Assisi to follow his path of poverty and love of all men.

So the Brothers went back to Assisi, to tell the others they were no longer a bunch of homeless drop-outs; they were the Friars Minor—the Lesser Brothers—backed by the authority of the Pope himself.

7. *The Sister*

WHEN FRANCIS and his companions got back from Rome, they were given a wonderful surprise.

The Benedictine monks who owned the Portiuncùla suggested that they would like it to become the permanent mother church of the new order. They said they had no wish to make him own property, so he should pay them rent—one basket of fish every year, caught out of the river.

It was a wonderful idea; new brothers could join them; brothers who had been out preaching would come home to it. Francis accepted it gratefully as a gift from God.

He had always been a familiar figure in Assisi, when he was a rich young man and when he was the Little Poor Man, and now when he was Father of the Lesser Brothers. Some of the townspeople pitied him, some were puzzled by him, some loved and admired him.

One of those who admired him most was a girl called Clare. Her father was a nobleman, the Count of Scefi, who owned a great stone castle in the mountains as well as a fine town house. She was the third of his five children; and her name, Clare, meant the Shining One.

Her mother, Lady Ortolana, was a deeply religious woman, and as a little girl Clare loved to pray, and to repeat to herself the stories of Jesus in the Gospels.

She grew up to be beautiful, with wonderful long fair hair; and talented, able to do the exquisite embroidery for which the ladies of Assisi were famous. Her father, Count Favorino, planned that she should make a rich marriage, to gratify the family pride.

Clare was about twelve when Francis became the talking point of Assisi. She heard her father and relations say how badly he had behaved to his father; but she was thrilled as she thought about his care for the lepers, and his hard work building the ruined churches. Sometimes she caught a glimpse of him as she passed through the town on her way from home to church.

Her heart burned with admiration for him. How wonderful it would be, she thought, to make a heroic gesture, leave everything behind, and afterwards give up the whole of one's life to the love of God.

She began to dream of it. Instead of making the rich worldly marriage her family expected of her, she longed to become a bride of Christ. Yet she did not want to join any of the convents that existed already, which did not seem to call for the sacrifice she wanted to make.

She longed to meet Francis face to face, to tell him her problems and ask for his advice. Only two people knew her hopes, as she told them secretly. One was her aunt, the Lady Bianca Guelfucci, and the other was her little sister, Agnes.

Now he was back from Rome with the Pope's approval, Francis was asked by the Bishop to preach in the Cathedral. Clare went to listen to him, and at last he spoke to her. He suggested she should come to see him at the Portiuncula.

The Lady Bianca agreed to take her. Francis left the settlement of huts, and he and Clare walked in the woods together while she told him she wanted to live her whole life for God.

Francis declared he was 'wishful to snatch this noble prey out of the reach of a wicked world'. He was so sure of Clare's strength of purpose that, after several discussions, he agreed to help her, even though he knew many people in Assisi would be shocked and horrified.

On Palm Sunday in 1212, when she was nineteen years old, Clare went to the cathedral with her family for the Palm Sunday procession. She wore her best clothes for the festival—a scarlet dress and jewelled belt, and a high headdress over her long fair hair.

As she knelt with her family, she knew it was the last time. They would be heartbroken. For herself, she was giving up all hope of earthly happiness and accepting hardship and poverty that she could hardly imagine. She was so overcome by her feelings that when the others went to the altar to fetch the blessed palms, she could not even get up from her place.

When the Bishop had given palms to everyone else, he came down to where Clare was kneeling and put a blessed palm in her hands—a palm shaped like the cross of Christ that she was taking up for his sake. It was a welcome sign to Clare that the Bishop knew about the step she was going to take and gave it his blessing.

That night, Clare got up from her room and crept through the silent passages to the kitchen. Silently and carefully she slipped out into the narrow street, where she had never been alone in her life, and made her way to the town gate. Bianca was waiting for her there. In the darkness they reached the woodland surrounding the Portiuncula and stumbled along the paths, trying to hurry.

Suddenly in front of them they saw a blaze of light and heard singing. Led by Francis, all the brothers were coming to welcome Clare, carrying candles and singing thanks to God for their new sister.

They took her into the church and heard Mass together. Clare laid aside her festival finery and put on the rough habit and rope that the brothers wore. Francis himself cut off her long, beautiful fair hair and laid a veil over her head.

Francis believed his Rule was going to spread to an order of sisters, and that Clare was the first of many. He was right: the Second Order of Franciscans, the Sisters of the Lesser Brothers, had begun, with Clare as its founder. Before long they would be known as the Poor Clares.

Bianca slipped back home, and in the early morning Francis took Clare to a convent nearby so that she would have a place of safety to face her family.

They were as angry and upset as she had feared. Her father, brothers, cousins, stormed and told her she was disgracing the family. They ordered her to go home. Her mother cried, and asked her if she didn't want a home and children like any normal girl. Her little sister Agnes look on wide-eyed and said nothing.

Clare stood on the steps of the altar in the convent chapel. She would not go home, she told her family. They could not persuade her or force her to go back. She begged them to leave her in peace, to live the life that was right for her.

Not her pleas but her obstinacy made them give up, and they left her alone.

Agnes went home too, thinking hard. She loved Clare more than anyone in the world; she did not like her family and the way they were behaving. She too had dreams of living her life as God wished, not as her worldly family wanted. She believed that with Clare to help her, she would be able to share her life.

Less than three weeks after Clare left home, Agnes followed her. She came running up the hill, begging the nuns to take her in and let her join Clare.

The noble family of Scefi were really outraged. A second daughter running away like this made them look ridiculous. This time they marched right into the convent and tried to drag Agnes away by sheer force. All the time Clare prayed to God to save her sister.

The kinsmen realised this struggle with a sixteen-year-old girl was certainly ridiculous and very unseemly. They stopped trying to force Agnes to go with them and went quietly back to Assisi, leaving Clare and Agnes to the lives they had chosen.

Yet what was to happen to the girls now? They could scarcely join the Brothers at Portiuncula, but they had not left home to join an ordinary convent. Once more the Benedictine monks came to the rescue. They offered Francis St Damian's as a home for his new followers.

Francis was delighted to realise that all those years ago, when he was rebuilding St Damian's, all the time he was getting it ready for the new sisters.

So Clare and Agnes set themselves up there, and Francis drew up a Rule for them to follow. Like the brothers, they were to be devoted to poverty and prayer. But it was different: they would not go out in the world preaching, but would spend all their lives in their convent. They would grow their own food, and what else they needed the brothers would beg for them. The sisters—Francis used to call them the Ladies—would spin and weave cloth and make the habits for the brothers, and they would embroider linen for the churches. They made a hospital to look after the sick poor and any brothers who were ill.

And above all they were to pray—for the brothers on their preaching missions, and for the men and women who would hear them and be turned to God.

When Clare ran away from home, she had a heroic vision of what she would do for God, giving up everything, carrying God's name everywhere, equal to the brothers in endurance and courage. She had not thought of life in an enclosed convent. But she accepted Francis's Rule as if it came directly from God.

Only once, when she heard that two of the Brothers had been martyred by the Moslems in Morocco, she burst into tears and said she too should have been a martyr for the love of Christ.

But if she was to embrace poverty and prayer, she did it on a heroic scale, guiding and directing the sisters. Every night, they said, after Compline—the last office of the day—was over, Clare stayed alone in the chapel for hours, kneeling before the crucifix, repeating prayers Francis had taught her. She became famous for her prayers, and queens and great ladies and bishops of the church used to write to her, asking for her prayers and for her advice.

After Agnes, Bianca was one of the first to join her. And after her father, the Count of Scefi, died, her mother followed her.

Agnes was her devoted helper; but after seven years they founded another convent near Florence, and Agnes, still only twenty-three, was sent to be its Abbess. For thirty years she never saw Clare; and this was her greatest sacrifice to the life of prayer and poverty, of which they were both such shining lights.

Sometimes Francis used to walk across to St Damian's to talk with Clare about the needs of the convents, and he would ask Clare's advice about the work of the brothers. Then they would stop talking about their own lives and talk together about the love of Christ for all men.

At the end of her life, Clare said: 'From the day when I first knew the grace of Our Lord Jesus Christ through his servant Francis, no pain has seemed grievous to me, no penance hard, no sickness difficult to bear.'

And she used to describe herself as Clare the unworthy handmaid of Christ and small plant of our blessed father, Francis.

8. All the works of the Lord

THE NEXT YEARS passed happily as the Brothers grew in numbers and tried to follow the Rule faithfully. They loved Francis and treasured everything he did, every word that he spoke. Brother Leo wrote everything down, and he called himself and the Brothers who knew Francis best 'We that were with him'.

Sometimes the Brothers did not understand that to Francis poverty meant owning nothing at all: neither the order as a whole nor any individual Brother might own anything beyond the shabby clothes he wore.

One Brother longed to have a prayer book of his own, believing it would really help him to pray better.

'No,' said Francis. 'If you own a prayer book, soon you will want to own a book of Psalms, and soon after that you will sit back in your chair and call to your brothers, "Bring me my prayer book when I call for it!"'

Yet he understood the men and women who did not join the orders, so long as they held their goods and money ready for the service of God. He always offered them his prayers and his help.

One lady from a noble family in Rome had been left a widow with two sons to bring up, and land and money to look after. She was worried about the future; but he encouraged her and gave her confidence. Her name was Lady Giacoma of Frangipani, but he called her Brother Giacoma—to show she would be able to cope with her responsibilities. Her house in Rome was a home for Francis and any of the Brothers in the city. Sometimes she made a sweet almond cake, and persuaded Francis to eat it. It is still made, and called Frangipani cake, after her.

Francis's prayers to heal the sick were often answered. One old woman showed him her helpless crippled hands. He held them in his, and they became straight and strong. She hurried home, and came back later with a cheesecake she had made for him with her cured hands; and she was delighted when he took a slice and ate it.

Francis always lived on the sparsest, poorest food, and the scraps their begging provided. In Lent he would eat nothing but an occasional mouthful from a single loaf of bread. But he was too kind and generous himself to turn away gifts he was offered.

'Courtesy is one of the attributes of God,' he said.

He took the whole world as a gift from God. The earth was beautiful because God had made it; the sun was splendid because God had made it; the birds and animals showed how God cared for everything he had made.

'Oh all ye works of the Lord, bless ye the Lord, praise him and magnify him for ever' shows how he felt, for everything and everyone was part of a world created by a loving Father.

He began to call all things Brother or Sister.
Brother Sun and Sister Moon were set in Heaven by
God; Sister Water cleaned and refreshed mankind.
He believed men had a great responsibility for these
things; and certainly no one who spoke about Sister Water could waste it while his human brothers
and sisters were dying of thirst.

He called his own body Brother Ass—lumbering
along, patient and hard-working, not always getting
things right.

Once he saw a boy with some doves he had
caught and hoped to sell. He begged the boy to give
them to him, not sell them to men who would
kill them. Then he stroked the doves gently and
soothed them.

'Oh my little sisters, innocent pure doves, why
have you let yourselves be caught?' he murmured.
'Now I want to save you from death and make nests
for you, so that you can live as God your maker
intended.'

The doves flew away and lived out their lives
happily in the wood, where the friars could see
them.

And Francis told the boy: 'One day you will become a friar!'—and that is what happened.

Francis loved all animals and was never afraid of
them.

One bitter winter he passed through the little
town of Gubbio and found it was being attacked by
wolves. One huge wolf, savage and frantic with
hunger, would seize small children and even attack
armed men.

Francis took the road to the forest, while the
villagers begged him to take care. Before long, with
fierce growls, the huge wolf sprang out at him.

Francis made the sign of the cross, and spoke quietly.

'Come here, Brother Wolf, I command you, and do not hurt me or anyone else!'

The wolf hesitated, then came forward and lay down at his feet. Francis carried on talking gently. 'I know you only behave so badly because you are so cold and hungry. I will look after you. I will ask the good people of Gubbio to put out food for you every day. But you must promise something: you must promise me never to hurt any animal or human being in the town ever again.'

The wolf sat up and raised his head so that Francis's hand lay on it.

'Brother Wolf, do you give me your word that I can trust your promise?'

The wolf lifted his paw, and Francis took it with his other hand. Then he set off for Gubbio, still talking calmly, with the wolf trotting at his heels.

The villagers were distinctly alarmed to see the wolf in their main square. But Francis called them and told them the agreement: they would put out food for Brother Wolf, and he would behave peacefully. Then he spoke to the wolf again:

'Brother Wolf, show me I have done right to make this promise in your name.' And once more the wolf put his paw in the man's hand.

Francis went on his way; but for the rest of his life Brother Wolf kept the bargain, wandering through the town, going into the houses, but never hurting anyone; known and loved by everyone, old and young.

The best known and best loved of all the stories of Francis of Assisi tells how he preached to the birds.

He was passing by a field just after harvest time. The sun shone in the blue sky and the field was full of birds picking up the fallen grain. On the ground and in the surrounding trees the birds were twittering and singing cheerfully. Fascinated by the happy scene, Francis said to his companions: 'Wait for me a moment while I speak to my little sisters the birds!'

When he walked into the field, the birds made no attempt to fly away but became quiet as he started speaking.

'My little sisters the birds, you owe much to God and you ought to sing his praises. He has given you liberty to fly, and clothing for you and your children. He feeds you, though you neither spin nor reap. He has given you fountains and rivers to quench your thirst; mountains and valleys in which to take refuge, and trees in which to make your nests. So God your maker loves you, having given

you such gifts. Beware, my little sisters, of the sin of ingratitude, and always give praise to God.'

Francis preaching to the birds was one of the most famous sermons ever preached, and many artists have painted it. But its importance is the way it shows Francis's love of God spilling over to every man, woman and child, every bird and beast, who were all, like him, the children of God.

9. The Sultan

NINE YEARS after Pope Innocent III had approved the Rule, five thousand Lesser Brothers were enrolled in the order. A festival took place at Portiuncula—they called it the Chapter of Mats because everyone made little straw mats or huts out of the green branches from the woods, for shelter. Francis preached to them, imploring them to keep the Rule and to remember they were all promised to serve poverty and not to be tied down to goods and possessions.

Then he said that twelve of them would set out on a special mission. Before this they had gone to the countries of Europe already part of the church. Now they would go to the enemy of the church—to the men who turned to Islam as their religion. He himself would go to the heart of Islam: he would seek out the Sultan, its leader and ruler.

The religion of Islam taught that Mohammed was its leader, and denied that Jesus Christ was the son of God. It was strong and warlike, stretched across Northern Africa, across the Middle East, and towards India. Even the Holy Land, where Christ had

lived on earth, was in the hands of these unbeliev-
ers. Armies from Europe had tried time and time
again in wars called Crusades to capture it from
them, but they had not succeeded.

Francis said he was going to the Sultan himself,
not to make war but to offer him the love and peace
of Christ. Yet the Moslems were fierce and intoler-
ant, and cruelly put to death anyone who refused to
honour Mohammed as the great Prophet. Indeed,
Sultan Melek-el-Kamil himself gave a golden coin
to everyone who killed a Christian.

Francis knew all this, and he truly hoped and
prayed that would happen to him. He wanted to
become a martyr for the sake of his Lord Jesus
Christ.

Francis and his companion, Brother Illuminatio,
managed to take a ship, and reached the camp of the
Crusaders. Their army was besieging Damietta, a
town in Egypt where the Sultan lay with his armies.
He was not able to get rid of the Crusaders, but he
was too strong for them to get past him on their way
to the Holy Land.

Francis and Illuminatio spent a while with the
Crusaders, then they walked slowly forward to the
Sultan's camp, up to the guard, expecting at every
moment to be put to death. They were seized, put
in chains and beaten, but not killed. Francis kept
saying 'Sultan, sultan', which was the only word he
could make the guards understand. At last they
were led into the Sultan's presence.

It was a strange sight. The Sultan, with a jewelled
headdress sat on a jewelled throne. The guards who
stood at his side grasped unknown, savage weapons.
Before him stood two dusty friars in shabby habits,
in chains but apparently calm and unafraid. They

greeted him as they had planned: 'God give thee his peace!'

Melek-el-Kamil was a brave man, and he admired bravery in other men. He was impressed by Francis, who was not afraid of him and who refused, when the Sultan offered to send him away with rich gifts. They talked together, and the Sultan asked them to stay on in his camp. He gave orders that they were not to be hurt.

Several times they talked together, and the Sultan listened when Francis talked to him about Christ. Francis offered to walk through fire, if the priests of Islam would do the same, to see who was unharmed. The Sultan thought they might not want to risk it. And when Francis said he would go into the

flames alone if the Sultan promised to become a Christian, if the fire did not burn him, once more he shook his head.

Perhaps the meeting was a failure, since Francis did not convert the Sultan, nor become a martyr. But as the two men, so unlike, talked together, they became friends. And when at last Francis left the Sultan's court, he did take a rich gift with him after all—an order from the Sultan allowing him to visit the Holy Land and make a pilgrimage to the Holy Places where Christ had lived.

Francis took a ship to the port of Acre, which the Crusaders held, and then he went on to Nazareth, where Jesus lived as a boy. He wandered along the banks of the River Jordan, and across the sandy paths of the wilderness.

He went to Bethlehem and saw the ancient houses that had been too crowded to find room for the baby Jesus to be born; and the shepherds' fields outside the town.

He knelt by the star which marked the place of the manger, in what was once a stable and is now a great church.

And for him, most important of all, he went to Jerusalem. Barefoot, in tears, he walked the Way of the Cross that Christ had trodden, and came to the place of Calvary and the Church of the Holy Sepulchre. He prayed that in the years he had to live he would come closer to understanding how Christ had loved all people, and what he had suffered for them. From now till the end of his life, the way of the Cross was never out of his mind.

He went back to Acre to take a ship back home. He was not well: he had caught malaria on his travels, and the burning sun of the Middle East had hurt his eyes, so that he could scarcely see.

At Acre, a handful of Brothers welcomed him. But there was bad news. While Francis had risked death trying to win over the Sultan, some of the Brothers back in Italy were trying to change the order. They wanted it to own property.

Lady Poverty was in danger, and the Rule itself was threatened. Francis made ready to hurry home.

10. *The Franciscans*

IN A WAY, trouble might have been expected. Francis himself, the Little Poor Man, had been able to live alone, beg his bread, enter a town and start preaching the Word of God, and no one objected. Some thought he was crazy and some thought he was the most sensible man they had ever met; but they did not try to make him change his own way of life.

When there were twelve Brothers, Francis wanted them to carry on in the same way, without the regulations of a tight organisation and still without possessions. Yet questions were asked about this group of men, and that is why Francis drew up his simple Rule and took it to Rome to be approved by the Pope.

Innocent III accepted the Rule, and he allowed the Brothers to follow Lady Poverty; but he said to Francis: 'If your fellowship grows, come back to us and I will grant you more power.'

It was clear at the Chapter of Mats that the fellowship had grown enormously; yet the last thing Francis had wanted was more power. Instead, he had travelled to the heart of Islam, seeking martyrdom at the hands of the unbeliever.

While he was away, the Brothers knew he might be killed and never return. They began to dispute among themselves. Now Francis was told by messengers who had gone after him to the Holy Land what was happening.

By now there were thousands of Friars Minor, in Italy, France, Germany, Spain and England. It was difficult for them to have no central headquarters, no mother churches, in these lands. Some said they needed monastery buildings and churches.

It helped Brothers preaching to crowds everywhere if they had studied books and knew what the great teachers of the Church said. So some said they needed books and libraries. Some felt that the Franciscans should become important men in the Church, and that it was a waste for them to remain the Lesser Brothers.

Many of them felt the simple Rule Francis had given them was not enough: they needed strict regulations which they all had to obey, laying out every detail of their lives.

They all loved Francis—that was not the question. It was rather that they doubted if they were good enough to follow the heart and spirit of his teaching. And while he had been away, all these changes had been made to happen.

Francis was very ready to go home, and he took the first ship possible back to Italy. He was far from well; the heat of the Middle East had been bad for him, and his eye complaint had not got better. When he reached Bologna, he was dismayed and grief stricken at the way the order was changing.

He went once more to Rome, and once more asked to see the Pope. There he asked that one of the cardinals should be made protector of the order. This was done; and together they tried to agree on such changes as might be necessary.

It was hard to agree on anything. Francis feared that any attempt to change the poverty of the order was betraying it; yet many felt careful changes were the best way of keeping the order alive.

There was no quarrel, no split between Francis and his followers; but the different paths could never meet. Francis and the first Brothers lived by the early Rule; more and more the Brothers who came later accepted the new Rule.

It was not what Francis had hoped, and the knowledge of it saddened his last years.

It may be that the changes made it possible for the Franciscan Order to endure for centuries, with thousands of Friars Minor doing great good in the world in a way that would not have been possible if the early simple Rule that Francis drew up had continued unaltered. Perhaps if it had not been changed, the Franciscans would not have lasted long after the death of Francis.

It may be. No one will ever know.

11. The Christmas present

FRANCIS was now nearly blind and very infirm; deeply troubled about the future of the order. Yet it was now he prepared a great Christmas surprise that was to last for hundreds of years.

He was to spend Christmas of 1223 with a few of the Brothers at a little retreat in the mountains, at a tiny village called Greccio. He thought back to his own visit to Bethlehem, not long ago, and the joy it had been to kneel in the very place where the Christ child had been born. As he always did, he longed to share this wondereful experience with everyone else; so he made a plan.

In Greccio there was a cave, like a small room cut right into the rock, and this gave Francis his idea. The Lord of Greccio, Giovanni, was a rich and powerful man but a true friend of Francis; and Francis asked him to help.

So Giovanni and his workmen made a stable out of the cave, with a manger inside it. They filled the manger with hay, and alongside it they built a simple altar. Then quietly they led a real ox and a real ass from his own lands and settled them beside the manger.

Meanwhile the people from the whole valley and from the mountain villages were told there would be a Christmas Mass at Greccio, and Francis begged them all to come.

So in the night time they set out, carrying lamps or candles and torches to light them on the steep and stony paths leading up the mountain, singing Christmas carols as they went. They could hear the sheep bleating across the wintry hillside. As they drew near, they could hear the Brothers singing, too—and then they saw a pool of light around the cave.

Then at last they saw the manger, with the beasts beside it, gently nibbling the hay; and at the altar, now set with candles, stood a priest ready to say the First Mass of Christmas, with Francis beside him to serve as deacon.

The people dropped to their knees and listened to the service. They heard Francis read the Gospel story—'And she brought forth her firstborn son, and wrapped him in swaddling clothes, and laid him in a manger, because there was no room for them in the inn'.

Then Francis told them he had arranged this for them, so that they could truly see the love of God who had become poor for the sake of all men.

As the Mass went on, everyone shared in the peace and goodwill that came to all men, and Francis was deeply happy to have given them such a wonderful Christmas present.

That was more than seven hundred and sixty years ago . . . but it has never been forgotten at any Christmas since. Soon, all over the Christian world, a crib like the one Francis had planned became a real part of Christmas. And now there are Christmas cribs in great cathedrals, in village churches, in

the churches in crowded cities, and in little mission stations all over the world.

Few people remember that it was Francis who planned the first crib; and he would not mind that at all. But when we look at our crib, at church or at home or at school, and give thanks for Christmas, we can say Thank you to Francis as well, for making Christmas live again for us.

12. The glory of God

BY HIS CHRISTMAS crib, Francis was showing his loving care for the ordinary people of God. In the coming year he was to move forward alone in a way that hardly anyone would be able to understand.

For many years Francis had prayed for two great and mysterious blessings; and since he had trodden the Way of the Cross in Jerusalem, he had never stopped praying for them. He begged that in his body he might share the pain Christ had suffered at his crucifixion, and that in his heart he might share the love Christ had felt for all mankind. Now, more and more, he wanted to have a time apart, to be alone to offer up these prayers.

One of Francis's friends, a landowner, had made him a princely gift—a mountain in the heart of Italy. It was wild and beautiful, with vast views towards the surrounding peaks and over the plains below. Lord Orlando had offered it, believing it was an ideal place for Francis to get away from the world and spend days in solitude and prayer. It was called Mount La Verna.

In those days, sometimes holy men kept a second

Lent with prayer and fasting in the autumn. It was called a Lent in honour of the Holy Angels, and it lasted from August the 15th until the Feast of St Michael and all Angels, on September the 29th.

So now Francis decided to climb Mount La Verna, taking with him his closest friends, the ones Leo used to call 'we that were with him': Leo, Masseo, Ruffino, Sylvester, Illuminatio.

They climbed towards the summit of the mountain, then Francis said he wanted to find a place apart. They found a rocky ledge almost split off from the mountainside by a deep chasm. They made a rough bridge over the chasm, and Francis crossed it. Then they arranged that every day Brother Leo would come to the bridge with a little bread and water, and call to him. If Francis answered, he would go forward and they would pray together for a while; if not, he would go back to the others.

For a month Francis stayed there alone. Each day Brother Leo came for a moment; and a falcon with a nest close by stayed beside him. He had no other company.

Then, on September the 14th, which is the Feast of the Holy Cross, Francis was caught up in an experience no ordinary struggling human being could ever grasp, no words ever make clear. Brother Leo wrote: 'The hand of God was upon him.'

Ceaselessly Francis prayed his prayer that God would allow him to share in everything Christ had undergone. 'Let my body share the pain that Christ suffered; let my heart share the love that Christ felt for the whole world.'

As he prayed, it seemed that all the earth and sky were filled with a blinding, piercing light. Then in the heart of the light appeared a great majestic figure, with wings like an angel, looking deep into his heart. And it seemed to him that the angel figure was in pain, suffering deeply, yet full of joy.

As Francis watched, he seemed to share that joy; then the light faded and the bright angel figure vanished. Slowly Francis came back to the world again, and as he looked down he saw on his own hands open wounds, as if they had been made by nails.

His feet, too, and his side were wounded. These wounds are called the Stigmata, the wounds of Christ. Nothing like this had happened to anyone before. Francis was in great pain, but he knew the wounds had been sent to him as a comfort, to show his prayers had been answered.

When Leo came, he helped Francis back to the Brothers; and he rested with them for some days. Very gradually he tried to describe to them what had happened to him.

Lord Orlando sent an ass to make his journey down the mountain easier. As the Brothers gathered round him, he begged them to care for La Verna and to keep the place where he had seen his vision as a holy shrine for ever; and this has been done. Then he said goodbye to the falcon and to La Verna, knowing he would never see them again in this world, and left.

13. The Song of the Sun

THEY TOOK Francis back on his difficult journey. By now he was very weak and ill, almost blind, and in continuous pain from the mysterious wounds that never healed. He knew the end was not far away, and he longed for it eagerly; yet he did not want to waste the time that was left.

'We have done nothing so far,' he would say. And although they took him to Portiuncula, he left it often to visit nearby towns, even preaching there.

When the next summer came he wanted to see Clare to say goodbye, so he was carried the short distance to San Damiano. Clare had a little hut made for him out of branches in her tiny garden, where he could lie among the flowers. She and the Sisters looked after him as much as he would let them.

One night he lay sleepless and in great pain, and alone. He began to put words together, and formed them into a poem—a poem praising God for everything he had made. Then he set his words to music; and in the morning he taught it to the Brothers and the Sisters. It is called the Song of the Sun.

Most High, Almighty, good Lord,
Thine be the praise, the glory, the honour,
And all blessing.
To thee alone, Most High, are they due,
And no man is worthy
To speak Thy Name.

Praise to Thee, my Lord, for all Thy creatures,
Above all Brother Sun
Who brings us the day and lends us his light;

Lovely is he, radiant with great splendour,
And speaks to us of Thee,
O Most High,

Praise to Thee, my Lord, for Sister Moon and the
* stars*
Which Thou hast set in the heavens,
Clear, precious and fair.

Praise to Thee, my Lord, for Brother Wind,
For air and cloud, for calm and all weather,
By which Thou supportest life in all Thy creatures.

Praise to Thee, my Lord, for Sister Water,
Who is so useful and humble,
Precious and pure.

Praise to Thee, my Lord, for Brother Fire,
By whom Thou lightest the night;
He is lovely and pleasant, mighty and strong.

Praise to Thee, my Lord, for our sister Mother Earth
Who sustains and directs us,
And brings forth varied fruits, and coloured flowers,
 and plants.

Praise and bless my Lord,
Thank Him and serve Him
With great humility.

The Song of the Sun was to be known and loved by the Franciscans, and by everyone who heard them sing it. Today some people think the most important thing about Francis is that he loved nature, and birds and flowers. This poem shows he loved God first and foremost, and nature as something God had made.

Francis stayed for six peaceful weeks at St Damian's, then good friends, bishops and noblemen, urged him to go to their palaces to be cared for by them, to consult their doctors. He was ready to live longer if it was God's will, so he allowed himself to be moved from place to place, and patiently endured the efforts of the doctors to cure him. But when it was clear that it was all no use, he turned back thankfully to Portiuncula, which was home for him and lay only a few miles from Assisi, where he had been born.

On the way he asked his companions to stop and turn his face to Assisi. Then, with his blind eyes gazing towards it, his arms stretched over it, he blessed the city that has been famous because of him for seven hundred and fifty years.

At Portiuncula he made ready for the end. Though he had given up all wordly goods, he wanted everything done decently. He wrote to the Lady Giacoma, asking her to come with candles and sheets and everything that would be needful for his burial. And, he asked, would she bring some of the almond cake he used to like?

Before the letter could be sent, there was a noise outside. It was the Lady Giacoma. She had arrived already, bringing everything he had asked for— including the almond cake. He was delighted.

'Bring her in!' he exclaimed. 'For the rule concerning women not being allowed here does not apply to Brother Giacoma!'

Clare was herself very ill, and strictly bound by her enclosed order, so she could not leave her convent to come to him. She sent him prayers and loving messages, but she was deeply unhappy at not being able to see him. Francis sent her a blessing and told her to be comforted as she would see him once more.

As a sign that to the end he was still the Little Poor Man, he had them take off his clothes and lay him for a while on the bare earth, a man dying without possessions. When he was laid back in his bed, he composed another verse to the Song of the Sun:

Praise to Thee, my Lord, for our Sister bodily Death
From whom no man living may escape:
Woe to those who die in mortal sin.

Blessed are they who are found in Thy most holy will,
For the second death cannot harm them.

He asked for a loaf, and he blessed it and shared it amongst the Brothers. And then the Gospel for Maundy Thursday was read to him.

Soon afterwards, as the sun began to sink behind the mountains, and as the song of soaring larks broke the silence, Francis died.

14. Saint Francis and Saint Clare

AFTERWARDS, the Brothers made him ready with the gifts the Lady Giacoma had brought, and they set out with him on his last journey to Assisi.

They stopped once on the way, at St Damian's, and took the body into the chapel. So Clare was able to see him to say goodbye. And when she saw the peacefulness of his face, she was comforted, just as he had promised.

He was buried in the Church of St George, which he had known all his life; but everyone knew that would not be his last resting place. Work began at once on a great church fit to house the body that was Assisi's most precious possession. In a few years it grew to become a fine building, with glorious paintings setting out the story of his life, and then it was dedicated—to Saint Francis.

Less than two years after his death, the new Pope, Gregory IX, who had known and loved Francis for many years, came to Assisi for a magnificent ceremony in which Francis was proclaimed a saint. Men knew then, as they have known ever since, that this new saint was one of the very greatest of all the saints. Centuries later, another Pope called him 'a second Christ'.

Francis might have drawn back from such honours, and he might well have thought that the great church was not suitable for the Little Poor Man. But it had to be big to hold the thousands upon thousands of people who have loved him in the centuries since he has died, and who have wanted to offer their own prayers in Assisi itself.

The Order of Friars Minor has endured and flourished. Because it grew so big so quickly, the simple Rule Francis laid before Pope Innocent III had to be altered; but still each Brother owns nothing for himself, and is devoted to preaching the Gospel and caring for the poor.

Francis would have been especially pleased, because after his death Franciscans were given the duty of caring for the Holy Places where Jesus lived on earth, which Francis had been able to see for himself when he visited the Holy Land. Because of his devotion to the Way of the Cross, and to Christ Crucified, the Franciscans made up the form of prayers known as the Stations of the Cross, so that Christians in churches all over the world can follow the Way of the Cross in their hearts.

Clare lived on, caring for the sisters and following her life of prayer. Not until twenty-six years had passed after Francis had died was she called once more to follow him.

Like him, she too was almost immediately, triumphantly, declared a saint. A church was built for her in Assisi, not far from the great church of San Francesco. The order of sisters she founded, under his guidance, still exists and is still known as the Poor Clares.

So Saint Francis and Saint Clare are acknowledged as saints, heroic servants of God, by all Christian people throughout the world. Many people ask for their prayers, believing that the prayers of two people who loved God so much, and who gave up everything for his sake, are sure to be heard.

Yet at the same time, everyone remembers them as they once were—the eager, beautiful girl who ran away from home because she wanted something she knew the richest and happiest marriage would not give her; and the Little Poor Man who tramped barefoot along the stony roads of Italy and greeted everyone he met with the words:

'The Lord Give You Peace!'